PRAISE FOR
MONEY LESSONS FROM THE WILD

"Joanne Lai's practical and anecdotal way of sharing 'money lessons' is a refreshing reminder and a good read for the young (and the not so young too). Her 'animal stories' approach questions the role of money in a light-hearted yet thought-provoking and realistic manner. Highly recommended read for young adults, and parents who wish to impart meaningful values and habits about money to their children."

— **Freddie Kang, CFP**

"This book is simply exceptional and brilliant. It clearly illustrates and inspires with animated stories, parables, great quotations, and the author's own life experiences. You will learn the foundational principles, key concepts, values and disciplines for successful money management and purposeful living. It will have great positive impact on your financial future if you apply the principles and values shared. I would want my adult children to read and learn from this inspiring and challenging teaching. I believe this publication will soon be a national and international bestseller. A must-read reference book. One of the best I have ever read."

— **Wee Tiong Howe**
Chairman, IPP Financial Advisers Ltd

"Succinct and relevant, a joy to read for all ages. While targeted at youths, the author has successfully infused her personal stories into a well-balanced guide for all. *Money Lessons from the Wild* shares—in a familiar, encouraging, and concise way—important messages in working towards financial wellness, while not forgetting valuable life lessons in resilience, personal growth, and social responsibility. Highly recommended for all parents and their young."

— Angeline Seet
Working mother and Total Rewards Director

"Articulating real live issues and addressing concerns in a way the local culture understands… fun yet straight to the point and packed full of useable tools and self-analysis. A must-read for everyone from amateur to experienced planners."

— James Tan
CEO, Tokio Marine Life Insurance Singapore Ltd

"An earnest and passionate nascent piece of writing to pass on the most important values of financial literacy. Thank you for sharing your life experiences and the lessons that you have distilled from them."

— Bernard Low
Teacher, Raffles Institution

"Joanne is one of the most knowledgeable, accomplished, and sincere financial advisers that I have had the pleasure of being acquainted with. *Money Lessons from the Wild* summarises many of the desired personal financial practices that an individual should inculcate. As Joanne rightly points out, one should start to invest as early as possible and financial competency needs to be ingrained from young. This book sets out to provide for the young the much-needed financial education in a delightful and engaging manner!"

— David Mok, CFA, MBA

"Every carefree child can grow up knowing a fulfilling and financially free life is within reach. Joanne Lai is well qualified to show the way."

— Patrick Tan, CFA
Managing Partner, Havenport Asset Management

"Want to learn more about finance but fear difficult terms? This is the book for you! It encompasses a lot of real-life examples injected into animal characters that are illustrated within this compact book!"

— Joycelyn Sng
Nanyang Polytechnic School of Design student

MONEY LESSONS
FROM THE
WILD

7 Crucial Keys to Financial Freedom at a Young Age

JOANNE LAI CFP

Financial Educator, Accredited Financial Counsellor

Candid Creation Publishing

Candid Creation Publishing books are available through most major bookstores in Singapore. For bulk order of our books at special quantity discounts, please email us at enquiry@candidcreation.com.

MONEY LESSONS FROM THE WILD
7 Crucial Keys to Financial Freedom at a Young Age

Author   : Joanne Lai
Publisher   : Phoon Kok Hwa
Cover Design   : Quek Hong Shin
Illustrations   : Quek Hong Shin
Editor   : Patricia Ng
Layout   : Corrine Teng
Published by   : Candid Creation Publishing LLP
                   167 Jalan Bukit Merah
                   #05-12 Connection One Tower 4
                   Singapore 150167
Tel/Fax   : (65) 6273 7623
Website   : www.candidcreation.com
Facebook   : www.facebook.com/CandidCreationPublishing
Email   : enquiry@candidcreation.com

National Library Board, Singapore Cataloguing-in-Publication Data

Name(s): Lai, Jiahui Joanne, 1986-

Title: Money lessons from the wild : 7 crucial keys to financial freedom at a young age / Joanne Lai.

Description: Singapore : Candid Creation Publishing LLP, 2017.

Identifier(s): OCN 999914541 | ISBN 978-981-11-4104-1 (paperback)

Subject(s): LCSH: Teenagers—Finance, Personal. | Young adults—Finance, Personal. | Finance, Personal.

Classification: DDC 332.02400835—dc23

To my family, my grandmother who has taken care of me faithfully for so many years since I was born, and for teaching me the virtue of saving and frugality. To my mentors who have helped me to grasp all the financial concepts.

For the young and the young-at-heart, you will be able to succeed in life when you focus your mind on the right thoughts and values about money. I wish that, regardless of your current circumstances or family situation, you will apply these financial principles to your life and succeed well.

Most importantly, I thank my Lord Jesus for the inspiration and the strength to complete this book.

CONTENTS

FOREWORD

"She walks the talk!" That is the first phrase that comes to my mind when I think of the author, Ms Joanne Lai. With financial planning experience from the age of fourteen and more than ten years as a professional financial planner, Joanne writes this book with the intensity and passion of a rock drummer! Joanne does not write concepts or principles from theory, she is sharing her deep convictions! She is unrelenting in unveiling the 7 crucial keys, the values and the practices of money management and financial freedom as if she is performing in the biggest gig of her life… and that she is!

'Many successful people start their success habits when they are young'—this statement in the Preface summarises the prime motivation for her book. Joanne uses her life experience of learning to save money from a young age and reveals the many lessons learnt about money management, coupled with quotes, and citations of current examples to develop the content of this book.

Money Lessons from the Wild is designed specifically to interest and impact children and young people so that they have a healthy understanding of the value of money and the need for money management, and will be able to practise the 7 concepts clearly presented in this book. Parents who pick up this book will do a big favour for their children by buying a personal copy for each child in the family. It will make a good investment as a birthday gift for a child too!

Reading through this book, I found a growing curiosity flipping through each section as I wanted to find out what Joanne was going to say in the next section, what animal story she was going to use to unfold the financial concept; from Runnie the Rabbit, who learned about 'compound interest' and learned to multiply her apple orchard and fed her entire family through many generations; to Sharaton the Sheep, who learned to 'share her wool (money)' so that the other animals in the jungle would not freeze, encouraging social enterprise! Joanne presents a very balanced attitude towards earning, accumulating, managing, and sharing wealth. Very important lessons for children to learn!

The layout of each chapter is simple and repetitive so that children can make easy reference to each section within the chapter: animal story—Joanne's personal story with application—questions to ponder—learning points. I really like that! At the end of the book is a summary featuring each of the lessons learned from the animals. This is a wonderful and creative way to reinforce learning through a visual of the animal and two key points: what the animal did and the financial principle learnt.

Finally, I wish to echo Joanne's words, 'Until you apply what you have learnt in this book to your daily life, you have not learnt anything'. I commend Joanne for writing on the critical skills of money management, especially for children who are going to face an increasingly uncertain and volatile global economic environment. I believe these 7 concepts can serve as a foundational base for their future success as adults!

Sam Kuna
Dean, School of Counseling (TCA College)
Marriage, Family and Child Therapist

PREFACE

"I wish I had met you much earlier, at least ten years ago! I'm thinking, what was I doing when I was your age..." These are some common phrases I hear from many people that I have met in my daily interactions, including my clients. Questions that I get asked many times in my meetings with parents are, "Can you teach my young or teenage children to be like you, know how to save and invest?" or "How young can my children start to learn?"

This book is for the young and the young-at-heart. There is no best age to start. It offers you some of the important money lessons which I hope will benefit you in your money management and life journey ahead.

Why This Book?

As the saying goes, "Money is not everything, but everything needs money". With the rising cost of living, most families require both parents to be working to sustain the monthly expenses. Our parents work very hard to make more money to sustain some of our schooling, tuition and extracurricular activities. However, they may feel shy or find it hard to discuss money management as they may not have been taught about this at school.

When Joseph Schooling's mother, Mrs May Schooling, came to my company to give a talk, she shared that her son had the desire to be an Olympic champion at the age of eight, after being inspired by his grand-uncle who was Singapore's first Olympian in 1948. Although his parents dismissed his aspiration then as he was still considerably young, Joseph strived hard and flew to the United States of America at the age of fourteen to pursue his dreams. He made history when he achieved Singapore's first Olympic gold medal in 2016. Many successful people start their success habits when they are young.

I started saving up at a young age and I managed to stay ahead of my peers in terms of savings, even while I was studying. My parents are not wealthy, but they taught me about money when I was a child. I achieved a five-figure sum in my savings account by the age of fourteen, while I was studying, and I managed to increase that to a six-figure amount in savings and investments by age twenty-one. With the advent of disruptive technology, there is no longer such a thing as lifetime employment, so it helps to gain an additional life skill by learning how to make your money work hard for you while are studying or working. I am privileged to have a mother and a grandmother who taught me many important money lessons while I was growing up. Those lessons have stayed with me until today and on my own, I learnt about investing and making my money work harder for me. With that knowledge, I managed to pay off the fees for my own university education before I graduated!

As a financial counsellor, I have personally met some people who have gone into bankruptcy at a young age (even before they could graduate or shortly after graduation). For some, it was due to their excessive spending resulting in huge credit card debts (sometimes their monthly payments were only sufficient for them to pay off only the interest) and having to keep up with their spouses' spending and lifestyle habits. For others, it was not entirely their fault; some were told to become a guarantor for the medical bills, business loans, or property loans for their parents / relatives / friends while others were asked to be the guarantor by friends for their credit cards.

I feel the compelling need to write this book to help people get out of debt and move into financial wellness and achieve the dreams that they desire while they are still young and employable. Also, I have read tonnes of books over the years and I realise that very few have little to no financial jargon. So, it is my wish to simplify finance in a way that is simple for everyone to understand.

How Is This Book Structured?

Most people like cute animals or things, so I have compiled a series of money lessons using animal stories. After every story, there is a quotation by a famous individual and I will share some snippets of my life and my personal journey of achieving financial success. There are also some activities and actionable points which you can work on after each lesson.

How Will You Get the Most from This Book?

Knowledge is power, but applying knowledge is more powerful. Until you apply what you have learnt in this book to your daily life, you have not learnt anything. I have always believed that once I learn a new thing, I will apply it within the same hour if not the same day so that it stays with me. Share the lessons with your friends and make use of the knowledge learnt. You will soon realise that by being a better steward of your finances, you will have more time to do the things that you truly enjoy without having to constantly worry about money.

As Steven Covey put it, "Live, love, learn and leave a legacy". I wish that the principles taught here will be meaningful to you and be a legacy which can be passed on for generations.

WHAT CAN MONEY DO?

If you could have a superpower in this world, what would you wish you could do?

Would you wish that you had some supernatural strength or some magical powers that could make you invisible or make you super smart to pass all your exams easily without studying? Or would you wish you could time travel into the future? Or would you wish that you had all the money in the world to buy everything that you wanted? I had always wondered what my parents were like when they were younger and also what I would become when I was much older. Since You Only Live Once (YOLO), will there be any regrets in my life that I wish I didn't have?

Growing up, one of my favourite songs that my mum used to sing to me was "Que Sera, Sera, whatever will be, will be". With the endless pressure my mum placed on me, I don't think she meant what she sang. She wanted me to grow up to not only excel in my studies, but also to be able to earn lots of money in future. Why is money so important? I had many doubts about myself and I didn't like to speak at all. I didn't want to speak to anybody as I was really very shy. I am an introvert. Why must I learn speech and drama and be streetwise?

"You are not cut out to study Higher Chinese, so you shouldn't be in our class." Those were the words that my primary school Higher Chinese teacher announced to the whole class when I was in Primary 4. I was deeply hurt by her words, but within me, I just wanted to prove her wrong. I have been labelled many harsh words since young and I always thought that, perhaps some of them were right. I was always wondering to myself if I would ever amount to something big, or just be another normal person going through life aimlessly. If you feel like you are not sure what the future path ahead of you will be like, don't worry, you are not alone. At least you are willing to pick up this book to learn more about yourself and gain control of your finances. Your self-worth does affect your net worth.

You must be wondering now, "Why is there a need to worry about money at this young age, since my parents are going to take care of me for quite a long time?" Most people need money. What was your first memory of money? What do you wish to buy? There are many choices that we need to make daily on where we choose to spend our money. You can use money for necessities like food, water, snacks, bags, or gifts for yourself or your family and friends. You will also need to make a choice as to what brand of watch (e.g. Casio) or shoes (e.g. Nike) to wear and buy. Some people prefer to give away some of their money to those in need or to certain causes like animal rights, orphanages, or other charities. The reward of having a lot of money is the freedom to be able to do the things that you love to do without having to worry about money.

I realised that there are a lot more wants and desires in this generation compared to when I was much younger. The convenience of the Internet and the accessibility of online apps and the bombardment of advertisements have resulted in a generation of young people who constantly 'want new', 'want fast', 'want the latest gadgets', and 'want to be esteemed' by friends for the lifestyle and the ability to buy quality products and goods. I didn't really have a mobile phone until I was in University and at that time, I was kept busy with a lot of school work. Although I had many wants, I worked hard for them by doing well in school and was rewarded by my parents and my school.

Money can be a means of helping you to fulfil a dream or a desire, or it can be a way of allowing you to help more people. Everyone has a different starting point in our financial journey and we all have different goals and dreams. Through this book, I hope to be able to help you achieve the following objectives:

- **Mindset**—Develop the right attitude towards the purpose and value of money;
- **Motivation**—Develop a life vision and financial goals (e.g. savings) in life;

- **Money management**—Understand where your money went to (budgeting, making the right choices between needs and wants and learning to compare prices);
- **Mastery of skills and talent**—Fulfil your dreams and help yourself to generate income;
- **Mentor**—Look for someone who can help you to achieve your dreams.

QUESTIONS FOR YOU TO PONDER

What do you need money for? Rank them in order of importance: 1–most important, 2–important, 3–fairly important, 4–not important, 5–least important.

Be honest. There are no right or wrong answers.

The purpose of this exercise is to help you understand your current priorities in using money.

Buy things that I like ☐

Buy food and drinks ☐

Donate to worthy causes ☐

Save up for the family ☐

Take care of my family ☐

Go out with friends and enjoy ourselves ☐

"You are free to choose but the choices you make today will determine what you will be, do, and have in the tomorrows of your life."
— Zig Ziglar

NEEDS
AND WANTS

Once upon a time, there lived two chipmunks. One of the chipmunks was called Chatty. As the only child in the family, she was often pampered by her parents. She did not have to worry about money and she could get everything that she wanted by asking her parents for it. Whenever something caught her attention, she would have to have it immediately. If she didn't get the things that she wanted, she would throw a tantrum at her parents or guilt-trip them for not loving her enough. The other chipmunk was called Cappy, but he was not as pampered by his parents. He was not born with a silver spoon in his mouth, but his family was not too poor either. His parents could provide for

all his basic needs but they were very frugal so they did not allow him to spend on luxury items. If he wanted anything that was deemed luxurious by his family, he would have to work for it.

Chatty and Cappy were very good friends. Then came the year for Chatty's graduation and Cappy was invited to her graduation party. Cappy wanted to attend the party but he did not have a set of presentable clothes for the event.

Cappy wanted to impress Chatty during her graduation so he invited her to go shopping with him. "What do you think of this suit? It's the latest design from JoJo Armadillo and I really like it a lot. Do you think I should get it?" Cappy asked Chatty. Chatty replied, "Wow, I have never seen this handsome and suave side of you before. I think it really looks very nice on you." Cappy smiled, "Uh-huh, you've only just realised that I'm so handsome? I haven't heard a compliment from you in a long time. I think I should really get this suit!" Gleefully, he checked the price tag. To his horror, he found that the suit was very expensive. He wondered to himself, "Where will I get the money to pay for this suit? This will probably cost me many months of my allowance. Even if I were to empty my savings for this, I may still not have enough! Maybe it's better for me to choose something else that is more affordable."

As Cappy was deep in thought, Chatty nudged him and said, "Hey, what are you thinking about? Just get it." Cappy hemmed and hawed since he did not want to embarrass himself in front of Chatty. After struggling for a while, he decided to tell her the truth. Chatty quickly assured him, "I am sure that if you speak to your mum, she will surely agree to help you pay for it. All you need to do is ask and she will give it to you since she loves you so much! If she doesn't agree, then I will lend the money to you. My friends will really think that you are so cool with this new suit."

Eager to impress Chatty, Cappy quickly ran home and told his mum about the suit. Immediately, his mum sternly said, "Cappy, I don't think that a young chap like you should be dressed up in such an expensive suit. And how many times would you actually have occasion for a suit like this? I hope you understand that it's not that we don't love you, but it is daddy's hard-earned money. It will take up a portion of the amount we need for our monthly household expenses. Let me show what we spend every month:

Phone bills	$50
Food	$300
Household expenses	$800
Classes	$200
Transport	$200

"Your suit is $300 which is equivalent to paying for our monthly food expenses. Do you prefer food to eat or a suit to wear? There is a difference between needs and wants. Needs are things which we cannot do without, but wants are things that you can live without. You can do without an expensive suit, but we need to have food to eat."

"If you insist on buying the suit, I think you can start to save up for it. Based on what you are given a day, $5, you need to spend $3 for food and transport so you can save an average of $2 a day. This means that when you take $300 divided by 2, you will take 150 days of saving before you can own this suit."

When Cappy heard the calculations and his mum's teaching, he felt that he should not only think about himself, but consider his family's needs more important than his own desires. Thus, he decided not to buy the expensive suit. Instead, he went to another shop that sold a similar suit at a more affordable price and got that instead.

On the day of Chatty's graduation, Cappy appeared in his suit and Chatty was extremely happy. She was very busy taking photos with her friends and she did not notice that the suit that Cappy got was a cheaper version. All her friends readily complimented him on how good he looked and they did not ask him where he got the suit from. He left the party assured that he had made the right choice of not overspending. He felt very grateful to his mum for explaining to him the family's expenses and for educating him on the difference between a need and a want. Cappy continued to exercise wisdom in spending his money and he became a role model to many of his peers.

"If you buy things you do not need,
soon you will have to sell things you need."
— Warren Buffet, investor and philanthropist

"Too many people spend money they haven't earned,
to buy things they don't want,
to impress people that they don't like."
— Will Rogers, actor and social commentator

One of my first financial lessons was learning the difference between a need and a want. A need is something that you cannot do without, like water or air. But a want is something that you may or may not need, but it is something that you desire to have, like a pair of Nike shoes instead of a pair of normal shoes without a brand name. I remember when I was growing up, my younger sister liked to buy snacks and she liked to buy more wants instead of needs. She didn't like to do comparisons at different locations near our house so I would tell her which location had cheaper items so that we could save some money even when we were buying some of our wants. As I was very insistent about inculcating the value of saving at a young age in her, she started doing some comparisons and she stopped buying expensive snacks. She moved from instant gratification to delayed gratification and she managed to build up quite a bit of savings over the years and now she has an impressive investment portfolio.

Some of us have our favourite K-pop idols and we want to be able to support them as much as we can because of their talent, their looks, and their songs. I used to scrimp and save on my food so that I could buy the CDs of my idols and the magazines with my idols' face on them. I remember that my mother was very kind and bought some concert tickets for me for my idol's concert. It was not cheap and she ensured that she bought two tickets so that my aunt could accompany me there. There is nothing wrong with having idols, but we need to be careful with the way we spend and how to differentiate needs and wants. I have not asked my mother to pay for another concert since then as I know that money is hard earned.

You can try your hand at classifying the different items that you have been spending on into needs and wants. Here's an example:

Needs	Wants
Food at home or for basic sustenance	Food in restaurants and snacks
Basic shoes (non-branded)	Branded shoes or limited edition shoes
Education	Concert tickets
Bus/MRT fares	Taxi fares
Coffee in local coffee shop	Starbucks coffee

While I am not against buying branded goods for better quality, a good way to save money when you purchase an expensive item, would be to buy it at a discount or when it is on sale.

Let's do an exercise. Compare the prices of some items you like to buy in three different locations within a few kilometres of your home. You can create a table, like the one below, to help you keep track.

Items that you like to buy	Location 1	Location 2	Location 3
Soft drink			
Fruits			
Coffee			

Let me give you an idea of how much you can save by choosing cheaper alternatives.

	Toast	Coffee	Hair Dye
Outside	$5 to $15 per day x 7 = $35 to $105 per week	Local coffee $1 per day or specialty coffee $5.90 per day x 7 = $7 to $41.30 per week	$100 to $200 for full dye every 2 months
At Home	$2.50 for one loaf of bread + $2.50 for spread = $5 per week	$6 per pack of 25 sachets of 3-in-1 coffee = $2 per week (assuming you drink 7 sachets a week)	$20 per box of hair dye every 2 months
Savings over a year	$30 to $100 per week x 52 = $1,560 to $5,200 a year	$5 to $39.30 per week x 52 = $260 to $2,043.60 a year	$80 to $180 every 2 months x 6 = $480 to $1,080 a year

LEARNING POINTS

1. Take note of the difference between needs and wants in your daily life. Before you buy something in future, ask yourself, is it a need or a want? This will help you to make better informed financial decisions when you choose to spend your money.

2. There are three main groups of people when it comes to spending money. One group will spend above their means, another group will spend within their means while the third group will spend below their means. You must learn to spend within your means or below your means so that you will have financial wellness. Intentionally be disciplined about setting aside money for Saving, Spending, and Sharing.

3. In a study done by Dr Joachim de Posada, 'Don't Eat the Marshmallow' experiment*, a group of four-year-old Hispanic children are presented with a marshmallow. If they can stay in the same room as the marshmallow for 15 minutes without eating it, they get a second marshmallow. Two-thirds of the children ate the marshmallow, while the remaining third were rewarded for delaying gratification. This experiment can be used as a predictor of future success—all of the children who delayed eating the marshmallow were successful by the age of eighteen. The others were less successful, with lower grades, poorer relationships, and

fewer had plans for the future or entry to university. You can learn to delay gratification so you can be more successful than your peers.

---

* The original Stanford Marshmallow Experiment was conducted by psychologist Dr Walter Mischel (b. 1930). This was a series of research tests on delayed gratification that were done in the late 1960s to early 1970s at Stanford University. Dr Joachim de Posada (1947–2015) was a motivational speaker, author, and consultant. He recreated the marshmallow experiment at Columbia University with a group of Hispanic children.

QUESTIONS FOR YOU TO PONDER

Now that you have done the exercises above and seen how much you are spending and how much you can save, ask yourself what you would really want to spend your money on. My sister and I did not go without our snacks so it's not about giving up everything you enjoy. It's about knowing when and where to spend your money. Think about alternatives. Also, ask yourself whether you can wait to get something. Sometimes, the price of items decreases after a period of time.

SAVINGS AND COMPOUND INTEREST

"I'm so tired of hopping for one to two hours daily just to get my favourite apples!!" exclaimed Runnie the Rabbit. She always needed to find them in the jungle where they had fallen from the trees. One day as she was munching on her favourite apples, she thought to herself, "How I wish I could move this apple tree to my house." Suddenly, an idea struck her and she started wanting to grow her own apple tree. She brought the apple core home and removed the seeds from it. After that, she took out the apple seeds in the core and looked for a piece of land nearby where she could plant her own apple tree.

Carefully, she buried the seeds and ensured that she watered the plant daily and protected it from any other animals. She did not know how long it would take for the apple tree to grow, but she waited patiently. After one year, she became the proud owner of her own apple tree! The apples grew big and juicy under her care. Runnie was amazed by the rate at which the apples grew. Her calculations revealed that the seed that she planted yielded an average of thirty apples a year from the tree. Runnie had always wanted to share apples with her family and friends. As such, she decided to plant another tree so that she could have another thirty apples a year.

To improve the yield, she provided the tree with fertiliser from Mr Boo the Bull. This increased her yield to an average of forty-five apples a year. This meant a 50% increase in the number of apples.

$$\frac{\text{Total no. of apples after fertiliser} - \text{Total no. of apples before fertiliser}}{\text{Total no. of apples before fertiliser}}$$

$$= \left(\frac{45 - 30}{30} \right) \times 100 = 50\%$$

Runnie thought to herself, if she were to plant another apple tree, there will be another thirty apples. The percentage increase in apples would be 100%.

$$= \left(\frac{30}{30} \right) \times 100 = 100\%$$

Let's take a look at how Runnie managed to grow the apples:

By planting more trees	
No. of apples per tree per year before any change	30
No. of apples per tree per year after planting another tree	30
% growth rate of apples by planting another tree	100%
No. of apples per year after planting ten trees	30 X 10 = 300

By adding fertiliser	
No. of apples per tree per year before any change	30
No. of apples per tree per year after adding fertiliser	45
% growth rate of apples by adding fertiliser	50%
No. of apples per year after planting ten trees	45 X 10 = 450

No. of apples a year	% growth rate of apples per year	No. of apples compounded in 10 year*
30	0%	300
	50%	3,400
	100%	30,690

*Figures are calculated using compounding rate of return calculator

As Runnie grew more and more apples, she managed to feed her whole family. She taught her grandchildren how to plant more apples trees and to work with Mr Boo to build an apple empire. Runnie's legacy lasted for many generations and she taught many of the animals the virtue of hard work and also how to grow more assets. They lived happily ever after.

"Compound interest is the eighth wonder of the world. He who understands it, earns it ... he who doesn't ... pays it."
— Albert Einstein

"An investment in knowledge pays the best interest."
— Benjamin Franklin

Compound interest is the addition of interest to the principle sum of a deposit. The simple way to look at it is interest on interest,

For example, you get $100 from your parents during the new year. Assuming the interest is 2%, the following shows how this interest is compounded every year:

1st year $\qquad$ $\$100 \times \dfrac{2}{100} = \$2$ interest

2nd year $\qquad$ $\$100 + \$2 = \$102$

$\$102 \times \dfrac{2}{100} = \$2.04$ interest

3rd year $\qquad$ $\$102 + \$2.04 = \$104.04$

$\$104.04 \times \dfrac{2}{100} = \$2.08$ interest

4th year $104.04 + $2.08 = $106.12

$$\$106.12 \times \frac{2}{100} = \$2.12 \text{ interest}$$

And this will continue until the nth year.

In the same way that Runnie saved some of her apples for her future and her family and friends, it is possible for you to make sure that you do not spend all your pocket money. You can save some of your pocket money and look for a financial institution which can pay a higher interest so that you can gain more savings for yourself. If you were to save money in a tin can, your interest rate is 0% per annum. If you were to save money in a bank account which pays 1% interest, you will gain more money at the end of one year. Similarly, if you can get a higher interest, the amount that you will gain will become higher and higher. Some of you can consider saving $1 a day. If you are unable to save $1 a day, you can save $0.50 or $0.10 a day. Learn the principle of paying yourself first before you start spending. If you save at least 10% of your allowance, you will build a habit of saving. After you have this habit of saving, you can then look for opportunities to grow your money at an even higher interest rate.

With just $1 a day, this is what you can achieve in twenty years (assuming 365 days in a year):

Savings a day	Interest rate	Returns compounded in 20 years
$1	0%	$7,300
	1%	$8,037
	3%	$9,808
	5%	$12,069
	10%	$20,905

If you can only save $0.50 a day, this is what you can achieve in twenty years (assuming 365 days in a year):

Savings a day	Interest rate	Returns compounded in 20 years
$0.50	0%	$3,650.00
	1%	$4,018.50
	3%	$4,904.00
	5%	$6,034.50
	10%	$10,452.50

If you can only save $0.10 a day, this is what you can achieve in twenty years (assuming 365 days in a year):

Savings a day	Interest rate	Returns compounded in 20 years
$0.10	0%	$730.00
	1%	$803.70
	3%	$980.80
	5%	$1,206.90
	10%	$2,090.50

You need to learn to pay yourself first—at least 10% to 30% of the money given to you—before you start spending. You need to set aside an emergency fund of at least three months of expenses to ensure that you can cope with periods when you need money urgently. If you are used to spending $2 a day, you will need to keep $2 (per day) x 30 (days) x 3 (months) = $180. Your parents work hard for their money but they also wish to leave some money or assets like a house behind for you to have an easier life. However, it would not be wise to squander all their hard-earned money.

I remember that when I was young, my parents would give me a daily allowance of $0.80 and I would save at least $0.50 as a bowl of noodles would only cost me $0.30. I would bring along my water bottle so that I would not need to buy a drink and this would save me about $0.20–$0.30 a day. Sometimes when I received more allowance for having to stay later in school, doing some household chores, or getting rewarded with some cash gifts from the school, government, and my parents for doing well in my studies, I would save a bit more. These small amounts added up and by the time I was fourteen years old, I managed to

save up approximately $20,000 in my bank account, which used to pay an interest of, averagely, 3% per annum. This meant that I had $600 a year in interest even while I was studying in school and not working. I am not working harder, but my money is working harder for me. It is not impossible to find some interest rates that are higher than what the normal bank offers. You just need to start young and start saving now. I read the book *Rich Dad, Poor Dad* at the age of fourteen and I learnt about assets and liabilities. Assets are useful and valuable things that have potential to grow in value over time. Liabilities are things which have the potential to drop in value over time. I told myself to accumulate assets and reduce liabilities.

I was inspired to start investing at the age of twenty-one by one of my friends. He showed me the power of compounding effect using a hypothetical example of two youths, Alex and Zach, who both wanted to be millionaires by the age of sixty. Alex started investing at the age of twenty-five, with only $500 a month at an interest rate of 10% per annum for seven years; and he left it to compound at 10% per annum. The amount of $42,000 grew to $62,000 after ten years and subsequently $983,500 by the time he reached sixty-one. Zach, however, only started to invest seven years later at age thirty-two. He thought that he had other priorities in life and he needed to buy a car first before he started investing. After seven years, when he bumped into Alex, he remembered his dream of becoming a millionaire by the age of sixty-one. So he started investing at age thirty-two. He would need to invest $500 a month for the next twenty-nine years, at a 10% per annum interest rate to reach the same goal.

Notice here that the total investment by Alex is only $42,000 but the compounding effect of 10% per annum for thirty-six years added approximately $942,000 to his initial sum. On the other hand, Zach's total investment amounted to $174,000 and the total compounded interest was $768,000.

When I saw this diagram at age twenty-one, I told myself, "Thankfully, I still have some four years before reaching twenty-five years old." Quickly, I started investing my first $10,000 and my first $300 per month and this portfolio has since grown.

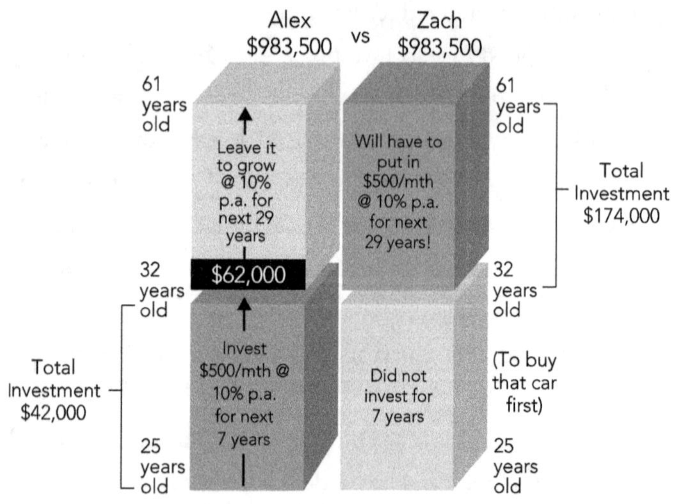

I learnt three things from this diagram:

1. I shall not buy my first car until I have at least invested for seven years.
2. I shall set aside at least 10–30% of my salary for investments and look for good investments.
3. If I am unable to grow my money at 10% per annum, I will invest for more than seven years to make my money work harder.

I told myself back then that since I was not earning a lot of money, I would need to save more; and even if I could not find something which paid an interest of 10% per annum, I would still be better off starting earlier then than later.

LEARNING POINTS

1. You can classify the things you own as your assets, and the things that you owe as liabilities. The more assets and fewer liabilities you have, the better your financial position. Remember: Net worth = Assets – Liabilities.

Assets	Liabilities
Savings in bank	Loans from friends
Savings in investments	Study loans
Books	Neglecting education and knowledge
Time	Wasting time
Positive mindset	Negative mindset
Good relationships with family and friends	Bad relationships with family and friends

2. The earlier you start saving and building up your assets, the easier it will be for you to achieve your target. Even if it is a small sum every month, save it and let the compound interest work for you.

QUESTIONS FOR YOU TO PONDER

1. Write down some of your own personal expenses on a daily basis and keep track on where you have been spending and what you have been saving. I have filled up the first row as an example.

Money that comes in	Money that flows out	Net cash flow
Allowance $5	Recess $2 Lunch $2.50	$5 – $2 – $2.50 = $0.50

2. What is your dream? When do you foresee yourself achieving your dream(s)? Being prudent about your spending habits may take you one step closer to your dream(s). Keep in mind what Confucius said, "Choose a job you love and you will never have to work a day in your life."

EARNING MONEY

"Hey Leo, what are you going to do this summer? It's the summer holidays!" Leap, his best buddy, exclaimed excitedly. Leo the Leopard replied, "Oh, I will be going to the forest to hunt for some food for my family. How about you? Where are your parents taking you to this time?"

"Sorry to hear that you need to hunt. My parents are taking me to another forest to enjoy the scenery this time. I will get to play with my relatives who are staying there. I am so excited! Ok, take care and see you in a months' time." Leo bade farewell to Leap.

Leo was the only one in his family who was capable of hunting. A few months ago, his father came down with an illness

and was forced to stop hunting. As they did not have enough food reserves to last through the winter, the family suffered because of the lack of food. Leo was still young as a hunter. He could not outrun some of his prey and he struggled to bring food home for the family. Nevertheless, being a filial son, he chose to continue to hunt and trained himself to run faster. The constant running and training required him to endure hardship for long hours and his feet were often sore by the end of the day. In the past, when Leo fancied eating deer meat, he would just ask his dad to get the deer. He did not realise how hard his dad had to work to bring the deer home. It was only when Leo himself had to hunt for the family that he realised that he had taken his dad's hard work for granted and he was remorseful.

Leo started to be more responsible and he started to make sure that he did not waste the food that he brought home for the family and ensured that his family had enough food for

the winter. When Leap and his family came back from their holidays, they realised that they had forgotten to prepare for the winter. They did not have sufficient food and looked set to starve through the season. Thankfully, because of Leo's excessive supply of food, he could help their family tide through a few days in winter. Leap and his family vowed not to be complacent in future and to make provisions for the winter in advance. Leap and his family became even closer to Leo and his family and both families supported each other. Leap's dad helped to nurse Leo's dad back to health by encouraging him to exercise and to regain his fighting spirit and strength to hunt again.

"Don't take for granted the time you have with your parents.
One day they won't be there anymore."
— WomenWorking.com

"FAMILY =

Father

And

Mother

I

Love

You!"
— Unknown

"Never take for granted your parents.
If you have parents that love you and are there for you,
feel blessed. There are so many people who don't know
that kind of love. It is an emptiness beyond compare
when you know that you can only depend on yourself
and have to realise your parents will never be there.
So if you have parents that are there,
let them know you love them
because you never know when they'll be gone."
— Unknown

Not everyone is privileged to have parents to give them money to spend and you should never take your parents for granted. While it is not always wrong to ask your parents for money, sometimes earning active income (e.g. working) is a good training ground for you to appreciate the value of money and diligence. You can also contribute to your family by helping out with your family's household chores or business.

You can look around for some areas where you can earn some active income while studying. In this way, you can gain some working experience while figuring out what you intend to do as a future career.

During my secondary school days, my teacher gave me an opportunity to work with two different professors from the National University of Singapore (NUS) and help them with their research work. I thought that the experience was truly eye-opening for me and this sparked my interest in mathematics and allowed me to broaden my horizon.

I also managed to get an internship during my A-level days at the Institute of Molecular and Cell Biology (IMCB). The internship gave me a hands-on experience and allowed me to identify what I liked and disliked about the role as my future career.

After my A-level exams, I decided to tutor some younger students. I also took up a few part-time jobs concurrently to gain exposure to working life. I sold some career guidebooks to students, helped to do some shipping orders of watches on eBay, and learnt how to be a dental assistant. I always knew the value of hard work, but it takes a real job to gain real life practical experience. Prior to working, I always relied on my parents to fetch me from place to place. I was very privileged as I seldom had to take public transport. However, working meant that I had to find my own way to the houses of the students, using public transport. My other part-time jobs also taught me how to interact with people, serve others, and how to be humble. I am thankful that I formed some very meaningful relationships with my former colleagues. When I resumed my studies, I continued to work to fund my own university education by giving tuition, even though my parents could afford the school fees. When I went to university, I secured an internship in a financial institution to find out if I was passionate about becoming a financial adviser. I learnt a lot from the internship and it has given me a fantastic head-start to my financial journey and career. The 'School of Hard Knocks' taught me to be thankful to my parents and to be independent. I learnt to be frugal and it is something which has stayed with me until today.

For some of you who do not know where to start looking for some jobs, you may consider what you are good at.

If you want to know more about your own intelligences and what you are inclined to do, you can try Howard Gardner's Multiple Intelligences Test (http://bit.ly/mulitple-intelligence-test). There is an Excel file which you can download and it will help you to calculate the scores.

This simple grid diagram illustrates Howard Gardner's model of the seven Multiple Intelligences at a glance.

Intelligence Type	Capability and Perception
Linguistic	words and language
Logical-Mathematical	logic and numbers
Musical	music, sound, rhythm
Bodily-Kinesthetic	body movement control
Spatial-Visual	images and space
Interpersonal	other people's feelings
Intrapersonal	self-awareness

When I was fourteen years old, I did this test and found out that my intelligence is Logical-Mathematical. This helped me to understand more about myself and I was selected by my school to participate in Mathematical Olympiad competitions and I won the silver medal. This also gave me a guide as to where I should focus my talents on. So, when I chose my University degree, I decided on a Statistics degree as I loved Science and Mathematics. When I had to choose my career, I also decided to do something that was related to my strengths. I have not regretted my decision since.

If you know what you are good at, then work on it to make it better. However, where you are not good at doing something, work with others who are better than you are in that area, so you can also improve.

LEARNING POINTS

1. You should appreciate your parents for providing for you and taking care of you. However, you do not have to rely on them to provide for all your financial needs. It is more beneficial to learn the value of hard work. You do not have to force yourself to work for the money. You can choose a job that you enjoy doing. Doing some work during your spare time, the school holidays, or after exams will help you gain work experience. You also learn to how to interact with others and learn to serve others. For those who are more entrepreneurial, you can make things which you can sell online or elsewhere. If you have a cause that you wish to raise funds for, the amount that you earn can be donated as well.

2. While money is important, it is also important to spend time with your family. The money that your parents provide for you can never replace the time spent with them, so spend more time with them and appreciate them more. Invest in the relationships with your family and friends as they are very valuable.

3. Find out what is your intelligence and work to improve it. Instead of ignoring your weaknesses, work with others as a team and look for people who can can complement your strengths.

QUESTIONS FOR YOU TO PONDER

Is there something you are good at? Or something that you really enjoy doing? Try looking for a part-time or vacation job in that area to start with. Doing something you enjoy will make the job more appealing and make you more open to learning new things. Don't think of it as a chore but as an opportunity.

THE CONCEPT OF PASSIVE INCOME

To mark the official opening of his store, "T-bone", Theodore the Terrier offered a special price of $0.80 a T-bone. The T-bone used to cost $1, but he gave a 20% discount to attract more customers.

Excitedly, Dex the Dalmation went to tell his dad about the discount. "Dad, let's go try the bones at the new T-bone store! They are offering a 20% discount. It's a steal!"

"What?! $0.80 for a bone? I used to enjoy a T-bone for only $0.20, three years ago. Sigh, this inflation thing… will turn us all into skin and bones!" his dad exclaimed. Dex felt that his dad was overreacting to the price. "Dex, let me tell you about inflation. Your money today won't be able to buy as much food in the

future. Things will get more expensive in future. It is a fact of life." Hearing this, Dex wondered whether he could still afford good quality T-bones when he grows older.

When Dex's dad saw his worried and puzzled son, he brought him to the Doggy Bank and started explaining, "You see, son, if I were to keep all our money at home, we will not have any passive income. There are two types of income. One is active income which means that we will have to work very hard to earn an income for ourselves. The other is called passive income where you do not need to work all the time, but the money or interest earned from the investments that we make will pay us some money so while we are working hard, our money is also working hard. This means that you will get free T-bones from the interest earned from Doggy Bank." Upon hearing this, Dex's eyes lit up and ears perked up. He wagged his tail furiously and asked,

"Oh Dad, does it mean that we can stop work and wait for free T-bones? Where does the free money come from?"

"Son, the passive income is not exactly free money and it requires you to do some homework to know where you can put your money for higher returns. Having said that there is passive income, I am not encouraging you to not work or be lazy, but I want you to learn how to work to build up your active income so you can have surplus money to build up your passive income. If you are only focusing on passive income and not working hard for your active income, it may be not be wise as you will not have any substantial capital to invest."

Dex grinned widely at the thought that he could have a lot of free T-bones by working hard and saving in the Doggy Bank.

So he told his dad that he would work hard. He also asked his dad to make sure that he would set aside some of his money for savings and make some investments to build up his money for the 'free T-bones'. His dad was proud that his son learnt very fast and applied his knowledge immediately.

"How many millionaires do you know who have become wealthy by investing in savings accounts? I rest my case."
— Robert G. Allen

I was exposed to the idea of inflation when I noticed that the food in my school kept increasing in price over the years. When I was five years old, it was only $0.30 for a bowl of noodles; when I was in secondary school, the same bowl of noodles became $1.50. I was thankful that my parents knew that the costs would be higher so they offered me a higher allowance of $4 a day. With that, I still managed to save as I only had to buy myself two meals a day in school and I did not buy drinks. I brought my own water bottle to save approximately $1 a day. During my junior college days, I was given $50 a week and I managed to save averagely $5 to $7 a day.

At the age of fourteen, my mum invited a friend from a financial institution over and started to expose me to the idea of investing my money for higher returns. He shared with me about how to make money work harder for me by putting it into a five-year plan which would ensure that it grew at a higher interest

rate than what the banks offered, at approximately 3–5% per annum, and the principal sum (what I started out with) would be guaranteed at the end of the five years. Seeing that my returns (what I get back) would be higher while I was still studying, I started to develop my interest in savings plans. However, I was quite risk-averse (not willing to take risk) and did not dare to invest in funds which offered a higher return (which meant I would get even more money) but was not capital guaranteed (i.e. I may not get my initial investment amount back). While you may not need to follow in my footsteps, a good way to start would be to find out what your options are.

There are a few ways to invest. One way is using bonds, which are similar to lending money to a person or a company. Imagine yourself lending money to a person. In return for the money that was borrowed, the person will need to pay some interest. For example, if you lent $10 at 1% interest ($10 x 1% interest = $1), then when the person repays you, the amount returned would be $11.

Bonds are certificates sold in order to raise money. There are a few types of bonds, namely government bonds investment high grade corporate bonds, and high yield bonds. Government bonds are like lending money to the government where you trust that the government will repay your loans back to you on time. Corporate bonds are like lending money to the companies that are owned by bigger companies such as the banks (e.g. DBS, UOB, OCBC), Singapore Airlines, etc. These will usually pay a higher interest because the company may not do well in some years so they may not be able to pay you the money back. This is known as risk. Investment high grade bonds are for those companies which have a better history of repayment while bonds which are high yield are usually riskier so they will repay you with a higher interest within the same time frame. There are also some companies that offer savings plans which consist of mainly bonds and some mixture of equities (more about this in the next paragraph) and other investments. Typically savings plans come with a guaranteed return and also a non-guaranteed return. The savings plans will usually consist of 60% bonds and 40% equities, properties, and some cash or other investments.

When you invest in equities, you are deemed a shareholder of the business and you can get dividends when the company makes money. For example, if you like to go to a bread shop to buy some bread for your breakfast daily, you may want to own the business and become a shareholder so that each time you see a long queue of people buying the bread, you can participate in the profits. However, you will see greater fluctuations in equities so your risk is potentially higher and your returns can, likewise, also be higher. For this option, the key is in choosing the right company to invest in, at a cheaper than normal price or close to its normal price.

The right way to approach your investments is by setting aside your emergency cash of three to six months of your expenses first before you consider investing. Do not borrow money to invest. Do not take the risk if you are not familiar with the investments, unless you have someone whom you trust to guide you through the investments and explain to you the nature of investments and the risk versus returns. When you do investments, you can have a mixture of bonds and equities, and this mixture is called asset allocation. As the allocation is specific to your goals and objectives and how you view risk, it will be different for different individuals. When you are young, you have a longer time frame to achieve your goals. So you can afford to take a bit more risk by putting more money into equities. As you start to age or reach your retirement age, you can reduce your allocation in equities over the years as you tend to become more and more averse to risk as the time frame reduces. For young teenagers, you can afford to take a bit more risk. You can start with small amounts like $100 a month. Investing is not only reserved for the rich and wealthy. In fact, we all have to start somewhere.

There are two kinds of investors, one is the passive investor and the other is the active investor. Passive investors prefer to put their money into indices, Exchange Traded Funds (ETFs), or funds where they do not have to actively monitor their shares all the time. They can either leave it to the fund manager to pick the stocks for them, or they can buy into a country specific or thematic fund.

If you like to be more hands-on, you can learn to do your own research before buying into the investments. You can either learn the basics of investing by reading more books or you can learn from some friends or gurus whom you look up to. You need to do the relevant research before you do the investment. As far as possible, avoid herd behaviour, exercise independent thinking, and dare to be contrarian. If you are not familiar and prefer guided advice, there are good financial advisers who are able to help point out where you can start your investments.

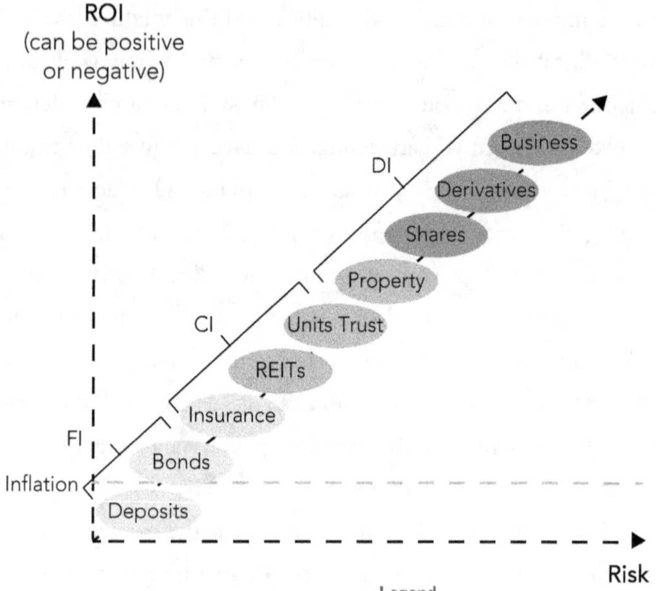

Legend

ROI = Return on Investment

FI = Fixed Income Investments

CI = Collective Investments

DI = Direct Investments

REITs = Real Estate Investment Trusts

Risk vs Returns

There is a line called inflation. The vertical axis represents the Return on Investment (ROI) and the horizontal axis represents risk. If you are only looking at returns without considering the risk, it is not advisable as you may be taking unnecessary risk for the returns. You need to be able to stomach the possible unfavourable results if you are looking at investments. If you are unable to sleep soundly at night, then the investment may not be suitable for you.

FI stands for Fixed Income Investments. We need to have money as deposits in the bank, typically, 3–6 months of emergency cash. However, the interest for these deposits are usually below inflation (e.g. 0.1% per annum) so we need to do some investments to beat the inflation. As mentioned before, bonds are debt securities and they are usually higher risk than deposits, but they can give a higher yield if you invest into the right bonds. Also mentioned before are the categories of bonds, namely government bonds, investment grade corporate bonds, and high yield bonds. An example of government bonds is the Singapore Savings Bonds (SSB) which are offered by the government of Singapore. You can start saving there with a minimum of $500 and it is liquid as you can redeem (i.e. return the bond in exchange for your initial amount of money plus the interest) in any month before the bond matures (the time stated at the start when they will repay the money invested plus the interest). The average interest rate of government bonds over a ten-year period is approximately 2.5% per annum. Other than the government bonds, you can look into investment grade bonds like Capitaland Bond which means that you are lending money to Capitaland to help them to grow their business and in return, they will pay an annual interest rate (which is also known as coupon) e.g. 4.3% per annum for ten years to you for lending part of your money to them. At the end of the maturity date, they will return to you the capital amount that you have invested. However, the minimum amount that you need to start investing here is usually $250,000 which may be a deterrent. The alternative to investment grade corporate bonds are high yield bonds which typically have a lower credit rating but in return for your money, they are willing to pay you a higher interest, e.g. 6–9% per annum. (A credit rating refers to a company's ability to be able to pay back its loans including interest when the time is due. The higher the rating, the more likely investors will get their money back.)

CI stands for Collective Investments. These are instruments like insurance, REITS, and unit trusts. The reason why I started investing using these investment vehicles was because it allows a smaller investment amount. The insurance plans, like savings plans which are offered by insurance companies, are usually 60% invested in bonds and 40% invested into a mixture of equities, properties, and cash. Some companies allow you to start from as low as $50 a month. REITs are Real Estate Investment Trusts which are good for collecting dividends (like rental income) from shopping malls, hotels, etc., e.g. Capitamall REITs, Suntec REITs. These are mainly real estate-backed securities. Hence, in addition to the dividends collected, there is also potential for capital appreciation (meaning the price or value will increase) if you know when to buy them at the right price when they are undervalued. Imagine collecting rental for a mall that you are part owner. You do not have to 'chase' your tenants for the rent as they will have someone to help you to manage the tenants. Unit Trusts are usually a collective basket of bonds, or equities, or REITs, or derivatives (Derivatives are usually contracts that get their values based on another entity's performance e.g. in a commodity derivative between a farmer and a corn miller, the farmer is guaranteed a certain price for his corn while the miller is guaranteed a supply of corn.) Examples of Unit Trusts include

Aberdeen Singapore Equity Fund which consists of a basket of Singapore blue-chip stocks (financially stable giant companies with good yields), and Philips Singapore REITs which consists of a basket of Singapore REITs. The average returns of the Aberdeen Singapore Equity Fund have been 9.3% per annum since year 1999 as of 30 April 2017. This investment allows individuals to invest from as low as $100 a month. So, instead of spending all the pocket money given to you, take time to learn more about these investments and earn more from your money.

DI stands for Direct Investments. Property is a direct investment and this usually requires larger capital amounts for you to invest in. Buying shares are like owning part of the business that you are interested in which will generate enough profit for you. For example, BreadTalk or McDonald's are businesses which you encounter in your daily lives so you may want to invest in their shares. You want to invest in things that you find easy to understand. However, if you are not familiar with shares, it is best to speak with someone or learn from someone who knows and understands more about investing. Ideally, the person should know how to read annual reports. For derivatives like options, futures and warrants, you will need more specialised knowledge so it is not advisable to start with those.

LEARNING POINTS

1. There are two risks if you do not invest. One is inflation risk and the other is consumption risk. Inflation means that goods are getting more expensive with time and if you do not grow your money, the value of your money will start to be eroded by inflation. The next risk is that you will tend to spend it instead of saving.

2. The faster you learn about your options for investing your money and growing your passive income, the less you will worry about money in the future.

QUESTIONS FOR YOU TO PONDER

1. Ask your parents how much they used to spend on a bowl of their favourite noodles when they were young. Now imagine that you were in the future and someone asked you the same question. That is how inflation works—the same amount of money will get you less and less as time goes on.

2. Before you invest, think about your own personality. Are you risk-averse and cautious? Or would you be willing to take big risks? Are you mentally prepared to lose your initial capital if your investment does not pay off? Knowing where you stand with regards to your own money will help you make more informed decisions about the investments you want to make.

CREDIT CARDS AND DEBTS

Cathy the Cat is the most popular animal in school. She is always seen in the most fashionable clothes, having the latest mobile phone models, latest games, flashy headphones, and the latest bedazzling manicure. All her schoolmates envied her a lot and they all desired to be like her because she seemed to have everything going well for her. Patty the Piglet also wanted to be like her. She wanted to get all the latest gadgets that Cathy had but she knew that she could not afford those items.

Patty the Piglet squealed all the way home and begged her mother Pigsy to get her all the gadgets. "Mummy, I have a friend who has a very cool phone. Cathy gets to play all the latest mobile

games and I am so sad that I can't be like her. She is always so popular because she dresses well and has the latest technology gadgets. I want to be like her. Why is it that, Mummy, you are not like Cathy's mummy who always has money to pay for all the best things?" Patty sulked to her mother. Pigsy objected to all of Patty's demands and tried to reason with her daughter. She asked "Do you remember your classmate, Penny the Peacock, who invited you to her house to look at her new entertainment system with surround sound last year? All your fellow classmates were invited too so that she could show off to them." Patty nodded and said that she remembered and she was very impressed. "But Mummy, Penny dropped out of school last month," Patty said sadly.

"Exactly. The reason why Penny dropped out of school last month was because her father did not have enough

money to pay for her school fees. Her father used his credit card to pay for the entertainment system and thought that it was possible to just make the minimum payment of the credit card bills monthly. However, the interest kept compounding over the next few months and soon, they realised that they were in huge debt. The system has since been repossessed by the shop as they could not pay. They also could not afford to pay for the school fees. As a result, Penny had to unwillingly drop out of school. To make matters worse, she needs to take on a few jobs, working twelve to sixteen hours a day to pay off the debts. Patty, I wish that you can have a good education and not have to work long hours just to pay off credit card debts. I love you a lot Patty!" Pigsy said as tears welled up in her eyes.

Patty felt bad and realised that despite not having the latest gadgets, she understood Pigsy's love for her and they hugged.

Patty was very touched by her mother's love and she decided that instead of being popular with the latest gadgets, she would just be contented with what she already had. She focused on her studies and eventually graduated with good grades.

"Running into debt isn't so bad.
It's running into creditors that hurts."
— Unknown

"Never spend your money before you have it."
— Thomas Jefferson

There are good debts and bad debts. Good debt can be a home loan which your parents use to fund the house. As the house has a potential to grow and appreciate in value over time, it may be a good debt. However, overleveraging (meaning borrowing excessively) may result in it becoming a burden and hence, being a bad debt. Bad debts may be credit card loans that charge very high interest.

We are constantly bombarded by endless advertisements daily. There are always going to be people who are richer than us, more fashionable than us, and cooler than us. If you are unsure of the difference between wants and needs, you will soon become a victim of various marketing campaigns promoting the latest gadgets, clothing, expensive restaurants, etc. Instead of putting the blame on the marketing campaigns and the shop owners, you need to learn to take personal responsibility for your money. You do not only live for yourself and when you get into the debt trap, someone must pay for the consequences. If you choose to run away from all the debts, your parents or someone who really cares for you will end up shouldering the debts. Part of good money management is to have consideration for others. Ask yourself how you would feel if the tables were turned. What if someone else in your family or a close friend was irresponsible with his/her money and you were the only one who could help settle the debts? Would you like it if your hard-earned money (through whichever means) had to be used to get someone out of trouble? Most likely, you will never see that money again. What if you didn't have enough savings to help and had to take on a job (or a second one, if you are already working) just to help this person? If you wouldn't like being in this position, then think about how your parents or family members would feel having to help you out of debt. This is why you need to have consideration for others.

Ultimately, the main considerations for you to attain financial wellness is to make the right choices and exercise control in spending. You can ask yourself if something is a need or a want before you buy it. Look at the Cornerstone Principles diagram. Consideration and contentment are both placed horizontally because they are about giving back to people around us. Contentment is about not being greedy for wealth or other possessions. Consideration is about integrity and honesty when dealing with people around you.

Capacity and capability are about skills, being well informed, and having emotional resilience (the ability to adapt to stressful situations or crisis). Character is about building your wealth based on values. If you manage to make a lot of money but you make it from cheating or stealing, then it may not be good for you. You may make a lot of money by cheating but you may be guilty or ashamed by defying your conscience.

Cornerstones Principles
Balancing a Healthy Financing Situation

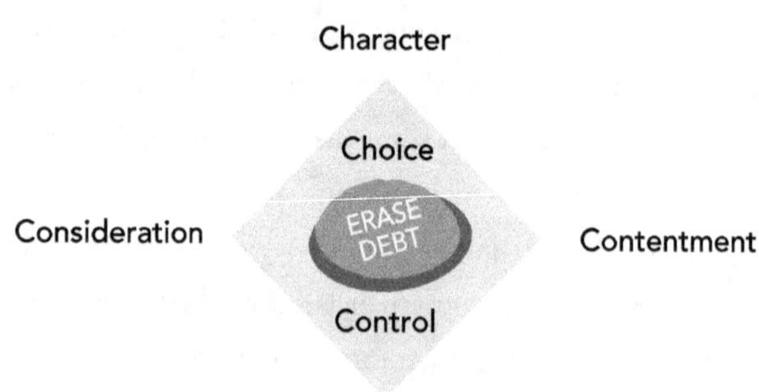

Staying Debt-free with the Cornerstones Principles

I have met some people who got into debt at the young age of twenty and have not finished repaying their debts even after they are in their forties. There were some months when the person paying for the credit card loans were making monthly payments which were only enough to cover the interest but not paying off the actual loan. It is going to take a long time to repay if the credit card debts accrue daily interest compounded at an average rate of 24% per annum (2% per month) and there are also finance charges if you were to pay only the minimum amount required.

In the earlier lesson with Runnie the Rabbit, I explained that compounding interest can help us to grow our money faster. On the contrary, compounding interest can also allow the credit card companies to make more money from us, resulting in us incurring huge debts.

For example, your credit card statement balance is $1,000 and your minimum payment due is $50 (usually 3–5% of the outstanding balance). You submit your minimum payment on time and make no new charges on the card. During the next billing cycle, the amount of interest accrued on the card balance is 2% x $1000 = $20, assuming you do not charge anything new on the credit card during the month. The minimum payment will be used to pay the interest charge first before reducing the outstanding balance. So, out of the minimum sum of $50, after deducting $20 to pay interest, there is $30 left to pay down the outstanding balance. The outstanding balance is now $1,000 – $30 = $970 (this excludes any late payment charge that could be imposed). If you do not charge any more spending on your credit card and if you only service the minimum sum every month, it would take more than two years to pay off your credit card debt of $1,000. This will cost you about $290 worth of interest charges in the process.

The table below shows how long it will take to pay off certain amounts owed and the amount of interest that will be incurred, if only the minimum sum is paid each month.

Amount owing	No. of years to pay off amount owing	Total interest (at 24% pa)
$3,000	5.2	$1,623
$5,000	6.6	$2,957
$10,000	8.5	$6,290
$50,000	13	$32,956

You would have noticed by now that interest charges take up a big proportion of your repayments. If you pay the full amount faithfully every month, these hefty charges can be avoided. Moreover, if you fail to make the minimum payment on time, your credit repayment record will be adversely affected. Your credit repayment record forms part of your credit report which is used by lenders to decide whether to lend you money. When there are consistent records of late payments, it might lower your chances of getting a loan in the future or you may be required to pay a higher interest rate for a loan. Hence, it is important to protect your credit record and avoid incurring credit card debts where you can, especially if it is for items you do not need.

If you were to buy a MacBook Pro and charge the $2,000 to your credit card and instead of only paying the minimum amount $50, you pay $250 each month. It should take you eight months to pay it off. However, if full payment is not made, interest is calculated from the transaction date until the date that full payment is made. This means that your first month's interest, under the interest rate of 25.92% per year, is $39.45. After eight months, the accumulated compounded interest is $347.34. That's more than enough to buy another 8 GB of memory for your MacBook Pro!

Sometimes, instead of a credit card, banks have a cash advance facility. If you choose to use a cash advance to pay for your MacBook Pro, $2,000 over eight months at 28.92% per year will set you back $388.39. In addition, there's a cash advance fee of 6% or $120, so instead of getting $2,000, you will only get $1,880.

So, what fees and charges are involved? The following table gives a good overview:

Fee or charge	What it is for
Annual fee	This is the yearly fee for the use of the main and supplementary cards.
Cash advance fee	This is charged each time you access extra cash. It normally ranges from 3–6% of the amount taken, subject to a minimum amount. This is on top of the interest charged on the amount taken, which is calculated from the day of the advance.
Late payment fee	This is imposed if the minimum sum is not paid by the due date.

Fee or charge	What it is for
Finance charges (interest charges)	If the outstanding balance is not paid in <u>full</u> by the payment due date (even if you had made a partial payment), interest is charged on your current purchases as well as on all subsequent purchases. Interest will then be calculated based on your daily outstanding balance at the rate of 0.066% per day (assuming an interest rate of 24% per annum) calculated from the date each transaction was made or the statement date (depending on the card issuer's practice). For cash advances, interest will be charged from the date the withdrawal takes place. Ask your card issuer to explain how interest is computed. The amount could be large if you roll your balance over an extended period of time.

Fee or charge	What it is for
Transactions in foreign currency	Transactions overseas or online charged in a foreign currency will be converted to Singapore Dollars by your card issuing bank. In your statement, you will usually see one amount in the foreign currency and one amount in Singapore Dollars. The exchange rates used to convert these transactions into local currency may vary from day-to-day and from bank-to-bank. There may also be other fees or administrative charges that factor into the final Singapore Dollar amount reflected in your statement. An explanation is usually included in the terms and conditions for your card. Ask your card issuer if you are unsure. For overseas transactions, there is also an international transaction fee (also known as a Foreign Transaction Fee or International Service Assessment) included. This fee is charged by the relevant card companies (e.g. MasterCard and Visa) to your card issuing bank, and is passed on to you. Check your terms and conditions to be sure.

Source: http://www.moneysense.gov.sg/understanding-financial-products/
credit-and-loans/types-of loans/credit-cards/things-to-watch-out-for.aspx

Decide Your Level of Living Means

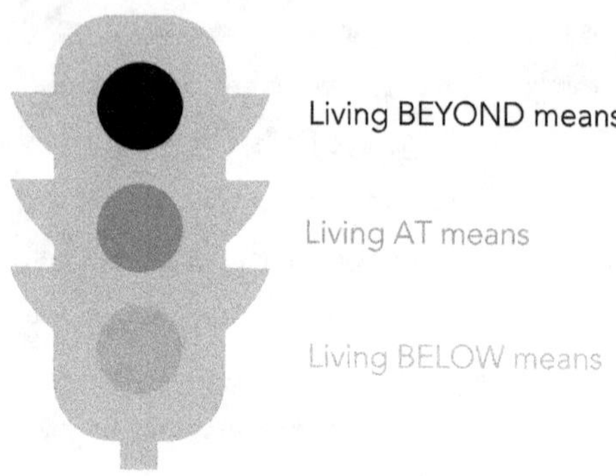

One of the most important steps to achieving financial success is to exercise self-control in your spending and your consumption. You can either choose to live beyond your means, live at your means, or live below your means. If you know that you really like an iPhone, but based on your current savings, you can only afford to have a simple phone, would you borrow money from your parents or friends first and go ahead to get the iPhone? Sometimes, we also can make purchases on impulse. We can look at something that we really like and just decide to buy it without taking time to consider carefully if it is something that we need rather than a want that can be done without. One good habit that you can practise is to pause and think for a while and ask yourself this question "Is this a need or a want? After buying it, will it make me much happier or it will only last for a while?" Most of the time, material possessions may only make us happy for a short time.

Personally, I have always been spending below my means. It is a conscious decision and choice I make. I am contented with the things that I have and I seldom like to purchase items to impress others. As Will Rogers put it, "Too many people spend money they haven't earned to buy things they don't want to impress people they don't like." I did not have a credit card until three years after I started working. I was concerned that I would be spending future money instead of spending within my means.

LEARNING POINTS

1. There are two types of debts: good debts and bad debts. Good debts are when you get loans which allow you to buy something that has the potential of appreciating in value in the longer term. Bad debts are when you get excessive loans which burden you.

2. If your parents give you a credit card, you need to know how to exercise self-control. You need to learn to live within your means and spend below your means. Do not spend beyond your means. If you have a credit card, ensure you repay the bills in full and pay them on time and avoid paying the minimum fees only. The interest charges are very high.

3. Instead of a credit card that allows you to spend future money, opt for a debit card instead of a credit card. A debit card allows you to spend up to the money that you have in the bank account instead of future money that you do not already own.

4. Never resort to borrowing or stealing from your friends and family to fund your lifestyle.

QUESTIONS FOR YOU TO PONDER

Have Loan Have Money	Yes	No
Yes	1	2
No	3	4

Which do you think is the best position to be in?

1 = Have Loan and Have Money,

2 = Have Money and No Loan,

3 = Have Loan but No Money, or

4 = No Money and No Loan?

Most people would think that quadrant 2 is the best position to be in, but actually most of the people will at some point be in the quadrant 1 where there are loans and also money at the same time. For example, our parents may have a home loan or a car loan and they also have money. Having loans may not be a bad thing; but what the loan is used for is important. If it's an education loan, it may be a good investment as it may give you the key to a better job or it may help you to learn more about something which you are passionate about doing. Needless to say, quadrant 3, having no money and yet having a loan would be the worst position to be in.

For some people who are unfortunate to have 'inherited' some debts from your parents' medical bills or failed businesses, you are not alone. There are many people in this plight but there is hope for you if you work out a repayment plan.

SHARING MONEY

Sharaton the sheep had the nicest wool in the whole forest. She was often complimented by her peers for having very soft and fine wool. One day, Harry the horse could not resist the urge to ask her the secret to her beauty. Sharaton replied happily, "The secret is to give." Harry was confused and quickly asked, "What do you mean? Do you mean I should give money to the wool-stylist to buy some expensive wool products or to cut a nice wool-cut? Can you give me the contact number of your stylist?"

Sharaton laughed and explained, "No, I don't have a stylist. A few years ago, I witnessed a frozen hamster in the field during the cold winter. I felt sad that the hamster had to die a tragic death. I

wanted to look for a solution that could reduce the number of frozen animals in the jungle during the cold winter. So, I decided to donate my wool to those in need. Every year, I will give away 100kg of wool to the naked cats, moles, mice, and those who do not have enough wool or fur to keep themselves warm. By giving, I realised that my wool became less heavy and I would feel more comfortable. In the past, I had a difficult time walking when my wool grew too fast. Now, instead of carrying excessive wool, the new wool that grows gets softer over time and I feel lighter and happier. I guess that's the joy of giving."

"Wow, that's so noble of you. You are really so admirable. Too bad I don't have wool to give away. If not, I would have joined you in this. I think this way, you get to kill two birds with one stone. You achieve the objective of caring for others and also help yourself to maintain nice wool," Harry exclaimed. Sharaton felt a little shy but her friend Sharry came and added proudly, "Of course, all the animals get through winter with her wool. She is very kind. Last year, almost everyone queued up for her wool and they thanked her for helping them through the winter."

"Sharry, you are making me blush. You also contributed your wool and helped me to organise the donation efforts by helping with some of the distribution so that the giving could be more sustainable," Sharaton said.

Soon after, Harry shared this beauty tip with the rest of the jungle animals. Other sheep came to see it as a great initiative and they joined in the effort to help. Together, they formed a social enterprise called 'Woolly Quilts and Jackets' to help those in need. This company grew tremendously and lasted for many generations as Sharaton's children and grandchildren and their friends and relatives continued to contribute unceasingly to the donation efforts.

"Our society has an obligation to invest now to
improve the lives of all those coming into this world,
not just those already here."
— Mark Zuckerberg, co-founder of Facebook

Mark Zuckerberg and his wife, Priscilla Chan, made headlines around the world when they pledged to give away 99% of their Facebook stock (worth about US$45 billion) over their lifetimes. The Chan Zuckerberg Initiative will make investments in private companies and the profits made from the investments will be used to 'advance human potential and promote equality' in addition to being donated to non-profit organisations. Zuckerberg gave two reasons why he and his wife made the decision to get an early start to giving away their fortune: "First is that we have a lot to learn and giving, like anything else, takes practice to do effectively. So, if we want to be good at it in 10–15 years, we should start now. Second is that any good we do will hopefully compound over time. If we can help children get a better education now, then they can grow up and help others too in the time we might have otherwise waited to get started."

Most of my growing up years were spent with my grandmother and she taught me a lot about giving. My grandmother has a very compassionate heart and she always makes the extra effort to take care of others. She taught me how to care for the less fortunate. There were times when I followed her to the market and when she saw strangers who looked pitiful or some disabled people on the streets, she would dig deep into her pockets to find some coins or money or get some food for them. She would tell me that these people are not very fortunate and if we can help them, we should donate some money to them. Although all this happened a long time ago, these memories are still etched in my heart and I have learnt to give when I see people who are in need.

I like what Mark Twain mentioned in his quote "The two most important days in your life are the day you were born, and the day you find out why." Our purpose and motivation precedes our need for money. Money doesn't give you a purpose. It's your purpose in life and your values that should guide the way you make money. The purpose of making more money should be greater than just your own personal needs. You probably have noticed that rich people like Warren Buffett and Bill Gates are also philanthropists themselves.

I may not be as philanthropic as Mark Zuckerberg, but I think that we can all play a small part in contributing to society. It does not mean that if you are not rich now, you cannot contribute. You can contribute your time to help through community service or do some other things to help others who are in need. I used to volunteer at MINDS (Movement of the Intellectually

Disabled in Singapore) and discovered that these persons needed companionship more than they needed money. You can also make a difference to the lives of others through your acts of service.

LEARNING POINTS

1. It is more blessed to give than to receive. We may not be the richest person in the world, but we can give of our time, talents, and treasures to help those in need. If you have some clothes, toys, or books that you do not need, you can also make it a habit to give them away.

2. Even if you don't have much money to give, you can always help others in their charitable acts. Helping a friend or organisation to pack items to be given away to the less privileged is also a good way to give of your time to a worthy cause.

QUESTIONS FOR YOU TO PONDER

1. Have you done any type of charity work or volunteered for anything? How did it make you feel? What did you learn from helping others? Remember, giving back doesn't always entail money. Giving of your time and your expertise is just as important.

2. Do you have a talent that you could use to help others? Perhaps you are good at organising events. You could use that skill to gather your friends to help out at a home, to volunteer for a bake sale or even to visit the children at the hospital. Ask your parents or a responsible adult for advice if you're not sure how to get started.

THE RIGHT MINDSET AND MENTOR

Taby the Tiger was the youngest in the family and all his family members deemed that Taby was too young to hunt in the wild so they would always put him in the garden. This would keep him safe from all other wild animals. In the distance, Taby could see that his Uncle Taffy ran very fast, targeted his prey very well, and was able to attack his prey within a few minutes. Taffy was known as the 'Fastest Hunter of the Jungle'. Taby wanted to be like Taffy and requested that he hunt together with his uncle. But everybody kept telling him that he was too young. Taby felt very defeated by their constant discouragement so he asked, "Uncle Taffy, will I ever grow up to be a hunter at all?"

"Oh my dear child, of course you will grow up and you will become a great hunter! Let me tell you, I started with hunting butterflies at your age," Uncle Taffy said encouragingly. He shared all his hunting expeditions with Taby and told the young cub that he could start his training in the garden. Taby took his uncle's advice and started practising. After a few months of skills training in the garden, Taby realised that he could only run fast enough for the butterflies but not for the mice in the garden. So, he asked Uncle Taffy, "Why is it that you can run so fast? I can't even outrun the mice!"

Laughing, Uncle Taffy replied, "Have you ever wondered why the animals you are chasing always run faster than you do?" Taby was puzzled, "Ermmm, what do you mean, Uncle?" Uncle Taffy

answered, "They are all running for their own lives, but you are only running after your dinner. That's the reason why they must outrun you. The next time you go hunting, just imagine that some other bigger and more ferocious animal is chasing after you and I'm sure you will catch the animal. Remember, you are a winner, you are a champion, and you can do it! Don't allow self-defeating thoughts to cripple you. I believe that you will succeed!"

"Oh, thanks Uncle, why didn't I think of that? I will do it. Thank you so much." Inspired by his uncle's words, Taby believed that he could hunt. The next day, Taby applied what he was taught and changed his mindset and decided that he would run as if he was running for his own dear life. He then thought of a strategy to

entrap the animal by cornering it, and in this manner, he managed to catch a few small animals in the garden. He had discovered and unlocked the power of a positive mindset! He realised that it was possible to have the right thoughts, feelings, and actions which would lead to the intended results.

Over time, Taby's skills improved by leaps and bounds. Soon, it was time for him to go into the forest to do some real hunting. On his first hunt with the family, he was able to outrun and catch a deer, an antelope, and a wild hare. He was elated and his family and friends were all stunned and amazed at how fast he could run.

From that day onwards, he became one of the fastest runners, just like his Uncle Taffy.

"Recall that thoughts lead to feelings, feelings lead to actions, and actions lead to results. Everything begins with your thoughts—which are produced by your mind."

"Wealth Principle: If you say you're worthy, you are.
If you say you're not worthy, you're not.
Either way you will live into your story."
"Rich people believe "I create my life."
Poor people believe "Life happens to me.""
— T Harv Eker, author of
Secrets of the Millionaire Mind

I have been an introvert all my life. I used to struggle with a lot of self-doubt and I always felt that I was not good enough. I was not confident of myself and was very soft spoken. I recall that when I was in primary school, I was so afraid of crowds and people that it took me forever to buy my food. I had a fear of ordering my own food, fear of heights, fear of the dark, fear of public speaking, fear of a lot of things. My parents were both very worried that I would be bullied so my mum would help me to queue up for my food. Unfortunately, she had to work and couldn't do this every day, so in the end, she resorted to buying bread for me every day so that I would not have to queue up for my food. She tried many ways to make me be more independent but I was just too shy. She would always say that I was only exam smart, but not street smart enough. So, she signed me up for many courses to learn how to speak well. She encouraged me to learn independence and learn how to be on my own to achieve greater things. Slowly, I confronted all my fears and, one by one, I overcame them.

We tend to speak to ourselves consciously or subconsciously. If we constantly feed our minds with negative emotions and thoughts, it will only become a battlefield of worrisome thoughts instead of a verdant garden of constructive ideas and things which can help us to achieve the next level of success. I have a mentor who used to ask me to repeat the phrase "I am good, I can do it" at least ten times a day. When I first started working, I felt very inferior to others and it was difficult for me to break through my negative thoughts and emotions. However, with the help of these positive affirmations, I managed to overcome the negative feelings. To help myself have a mindset that attracts success, I also read books like *Think and*

Grow Rich by Napoleon Hill and the *Secrets of the Millionaire Mind* by T Harv Eker. These books have inspired me greatly. Napoleon Hill's secret is, "Whatever the mind can conceive and believe, it can achieve with positive mental attitude." I truly believe that the first step to achieving success is to have a positive mindset and think as if you have already achieved the success.

I have been blessed to have many good mentors who have helped me substantially and I managed to learn more things at a faster pace because of their experience. They have gone through much more in their lives, whether success or failure, and their invaluable insights and their willingness to speak the truth, in the right positive spirit, has helped me a lot over the years. I am very grateful to my mentors.

LEARNING POINTS

1. Your daily thoughts will have a huge impact on your life. If you have positive thoughts and you act to achieve the goals you have set, you will be able to have a more fulfilled life. As T Harv Eker mentioned, "thoughts lead to feelings, feelings lead to actions, and actions lead to results". Once you have a higher purpose than yourself, you will be motivated in life and be able to contribute to others as well.

2. It is good to learn from your own experience, but it is better to learn from other people's experiences. When you find a good mentor, you will learn more and you can leverage on their experience to accelerate your growth. If you are unable to find a mentor, you can read books by a person that you look up to and find out how they achieved their success.

QUESTIONS FOR YOU TO PONDER

Is there someone whom you can be accountable to? Or is there someone whom you look up to? Or someone whom you think can speak the truth in your life and be willing to see you through the different stages of your life? You can start to look for a mentor who can help you to accelerate your growth.

Qualities of a Good Mentor	Qualities of a Good Mentee	Names of the people you look up to and what values they possess
Always willing to teach	Always willing to learn	
Capable	Able to apply knowledge learnt	
Intelligent	Grateful to the mentor	
Talented	Enthusiastic	
Generous to share	Generous to share	

WHAT CAN ANIMALS TEACH YOU ABOUT MONEY?

In the animal stories, we have looked at a number of characters and how their prudence allowed them to achieve financial success. Likewise, we have also looked at some animal characters who did not do too well because of their lack of knowledge about credit cards.

CHATTY THE CHIPMUNK

What Did She Do?
She was an only child and got everything she wanted from her parents.

Financial Principles Learnt
While we can rely on our parents to provide, it is important to learn to manage our own money as well.

CAPPY THE CHIPMUNK

What Did He Do?
He was eager to impress his friend Chatty and was willing to pay a price to impress others but he decided to get something more affordable.

Financial Principles Learnt
Budgeting is important and there is a difference between needs and wants. By making comparisons, you can get a better deal for a lower cost.

RUNNIE THE RABBIT

What Did She Do?

She found a way to grow multiple apples with a seed capital. With the help of her friend Mr Boo the Bull, she managed to accelerate the growth of her apple empire to grow more apples within the same given time.

Financial Principles Learnt

You may think that your savings are not a lot right now, but when you can save some money daily, there is a compounding effect.

MR BOO THE BULL

What Did He Do?

His fertilisers played a supporting role which was fundamental to the growth of the apples. Mr Boo's role is like that of a bank or a financial institution.

Financial Principles Learnt

Savings alone can get you somewhere. However, when you put your money into a bank or a financial institution which offers higher interest rates, the compounding effect will be greater.

LEO THE LEOPARD

What Did He Do?

He used to have everything he wanted when his dad was healthy. Due to his dad's ill health, Leo had to step up into the role of hunter for the family. He worked hard and ensured that he had enough food for the winter. He even had enough food for his friend Leap and his family who did not store up any food for the winter.

Financial Principles Learnt

Anyone can fall ill. We should not depend on only one person to earn an income. You can start by finding some meaningful work to do during your vacation. This will gain you some valuable work experience and help with some family expenses. If your family does not need the money, save your earnings or share them with the underprivileged.

LEAP THE LEOPARD

What Did He Do?

He was happy to be able to go on vacation and forgot about storing up food for the winter. He later realised that it is important not to be complacent and to ensure that he and the family had reserves for the winter months.

Financial Principles Learnt

When we are too complacent and forget to save up, and unforseen events occur, the family may be in a catastrophic situation. Remember to store up your reserves for a rainy day.

DEX THE DALMATIAN

What Did He Do?

He did not know about money. His dad taught him about inflation and where to 'grow' his money for more passive income streams.

Financial Principles Learnt

There are two risks that individuals face: inflation risk and consumption risk. Things will inevitably get more expensive over the years and the value of your money will shrink with time if you do not invest it in the appropriate places. Consumption risk is where you spend your money instead of saving it for future purposes.

DEX'S DAD

What Did He Do?

He was knowledgeable about passive income and he wanted to teach his son, Dex, at a young age to build up his passive income streams.

Financial Principles Learnt

Parents have a role to play in teaching us about money, but we should also rely on other sources (friends, books, newspapers, etc.) to learn how to build up passive income streams.

CATHY THE CAT

What Did She Do?

She was the most popular as she was always seen carrying the latest gadgets and items.

Financial Principles Learnt

In our daily lives, there are people who seem to be very popular and successful. If you have the wealth and the means to pay for the latest gadgets, you can aim to have a lifestyle like them and chase after the latest items. However, if you do not have the resources to build a lifestyle, it is better for you to be contented with what you have instead of always looking to buy the latest and best of everything.

PENNY THE PEACOCK

What Did She Do?

She liked to impress her friends so asked her father to buy a surround-sound entertainment system. In so doing, she got her father into debt. She then had to drop out of school and work.

Financial Principles Learnt

Start to think about ways to spend within your means instead of spending beyond your means.

PENNY'S FATHER

What Did He Do?

He loved his daughter and wanted to give her the best. However, he was unaware of the fees or charges associated with credit cards. He ended up spending his future money and having to pay the debts for a long time due to the compounded interest.

Financial Principles Learnt

Try not to have a credit card at a young age. You can have a debit card instead. For those who have a credit card, remember to spend wisely and pay up all the bills in full and on time. Do not only pay the minimum amount or just above the minimum amount.

PATTY THE PIGLET

What Did She Do?

Patty envied Cathy for having a lot of possessions and being popular. She wanted to be like Cathy. However, she soon realised that material wealth and popularity were not the most important things.

Financial Principles Learnt

You can have a lot of possessions in life but you should not place your value on what you possess.

PIGSY, MUM OF PATTY

What Did She Do?

Pigsy wanted her daughter to learn about Penny's plight to teach her the value of money.

Financial Principles Learnt

You can learn from other people's experiences. You do not have to get into debt before you understand about the perils that it entails.

SHARATON THE SHEEP

What Did She Do?

She had a compassionate heart and wanted to help those in need. She was humble and very sincere about her intentions and made it a point to assist those around her.

Financial Principles Learnt

While we save money and buy more things for ourselves, take some time to reflect on how we can be a blessing to the people around us. We can do that by sharing resources and giving to our family members, friends or relatives, or the underprivileged.

HARRY THE HORSE

What Did He Do?

He was envious of how Sharaton looked and wondered how he could have a nice image as well. He was surprised to find out that Sharaton's giving nature was the key to her beauty.

Financial Principles Learnt

Rich and successful people like the Zuckerbergs, Bill Gates, and Warren Buffett are givers. They have contributed a lot of their wealth and resources to helping others. Giving does not have to be in the form of a lot of money; you can start with small amounts.

SHARRY THE SHEEP

What Did She Do?

She was supportive of Sharaton's charitable efforts. Her willingness to contribute to her friend's endeavours is admirable.

Financial Principles Learnt

If you are not sure how to start giving, you can support someone else's efforts. There are already quite a lot of charities available which support different causes. If you like animals, you can donate to the SPCA or other animal organisations. You can also contribute by donating clothes or things or giving of your time or skills to help others.

TABY THE TIGER

What Did He Do?

He felt inferior and doubted if he could succeed in hunting. His family members and friends did not help. His uncle, Taffy, groomed him, by first changing his mindset and helping him to believe that he could succeed. Taby eventually became a very good hunter.

Financial Principles Learnt

Sometimes we feel inferior when we are not sure what our capabilities are. To be successful, you need to first change your mindset, from one that is self-defeating to one that is self-motivating. Then you can learn and acquire knowledge. A positive can-do attitude is fundamental to attracting success.

TAFFY THE TIGER

What Did He Do?

Taffy was a successful hunter who put in a lot of time and effort to build up his skills. He believed in Taby when no one else would.

Financial Principles Learnt

If you are unsure of how to get to your next level of success, identify some people whom you trust to guide and lead you to your goal. A mentor is usually very busy so you need to be a good mentee.

QUESTIONS FOR YOU TO PONDER

1. Which of these characters do you see around you?

2. Which of these characters can you relate to most?

3. Which character do you admire most, and why?

4. Which character do you dislike most, and why?

5. If you could be like one of these characters, which one would you prefer to be?

AFTERWORD

While reading this book, I hope that you can relate to some of the animal characters in the stories. You should be aware by now that merely reading this book will not automatically make you very rich. It depends on what actions you are going to take to achieve the goals and dreams of your life.

After each story, there is a quote that I hope will inspire you. There are also some exercises which I hope you can do to reinforce the money concepts. I have shared a bit about my personal life to encourage you and assure you that you are not alone in this journey. Although no two families are the same, I believe that the money lessons are universal. Here are some suggestions for your

- Think about the needs and wants in your life.
- Do a budget for yourself.
- Start setting aside an amount to save daily.
- Look for a place to put your money so you can earn higher interest and watch the compounding effect.
- Build up your knowledge about the different sources of income.
- Find some work to do during your vacation to know that earning money is not easy.
- Save up some three to six months of emergency cash for rainy days.
- Grow your money at least on par with inflation or above the inflation rate.
- Spend within your means and do not incur any credit card debts. Do not borrow from others.
- Be grateful to your parents.
- Share your time, talent, and treasures with the underprivileged.
- Adopt a positive mindset to attract wealth and success.
- Be willing to learn from mentors.

In the decade of my being a Certified Financial Planner, I discovered that a lot of people start very excitedly about their financial plan. Unfortunately, their enthusiasm for budgeting slowly fizzles out due to a lack of discipline and time. It is important for you to know that your financial destiny lies in your own hands and you need to spend some time on managing your money.

I have been conducting many financial talks over the years. If you are keen to get some financial lessons or financial tuition classes, look out for my upcoming talks which will help you to follow through and stay focused on achieving your goals. You can find out about these at: **https://acts-tensive-wealth-academy.com**.

Last but not least, I thank you for investing your time in this book. May it bless you and your family in the years ahead.

To your success and significance,
Joanne

GOAL SETTING

Use the following template to help you set the goals that will lead you to financial success. This SMARTER Goals template by Duncan Haughey may also be downloaded from http://bit.ly/smarter-goals-setting.

SETTING SMARTER GOALS IN 7 EASY STEPS

Name	
Goal	
Date	
Reason this goal is important to me	

Step	1
Concept	**Specific** Exactly what is it you want to achieve in your business or personal life? A good goal statement explains the what, why, who, where, and when of a goal. If your goal statement is vague, you will find it hard to achieve because it will be difficult to define success.
Description	

Step	2
Concept	**<u>M</u>easurable** You must be able to track progress and measure the result of your goal. A good goal statement answers the question, how much or how many. How will I know when I have achieved my goal?
Description	

Step	3
Concept	**<u>A</u>greed** Your goal must be relevant to your stakeholders and agreed with them. Examples of people to agree your goal with are your line manager, employees and customers.
Description	

Step	4
Concept	**R**ealistic Your goal should be stretching, but realistic and relevant to you and your company. Make sure the actions you need to take to achieve your goal are things within your control. Is your goal achievable?
Description	

Step	5
Concept	**T**ime-bound Goals must have a deadline. A good goal statement will answer the question, when will I achieve my goal? Without time limits, it's easy to put goals off and leave them to die. As well as a deadline, it's a good idea to set some short-term milestones along the way to help you measure progress.
Description	

Step	6
Concept	**<u>E</u>thical** Goals must sit comfortably within your moral compass. Most people resist acting unethically. Set goals that meet a high ethical standard.
Description	

Step	7
Concept	**<u>R</u>ecorded** Always write down your goal before you start working towards it. Written goals are visible and have a greater chance of success. The recording is necessary for the planning, monitoring and reviewing of progress.
Description	

Here is an example:

1. Specific

    I want to save $1,000.

2. Measurable

    I will save $2 a day.

3. Agreed with your friends/parents

    I will inform my mother/father that I will save $1,000

4. Realistic

    Based on what I have been saving daily, I should be able to comfortably save $2 a day.

5. Time-bound

    I want to achieve this goal in twelve months' time.

6. Ethical

    I will not borrow money from my friends or steal money to achieve my goals.

7. Recorded

    I will write down this goal and paste it on my mirror or somewhere prominent as a constant reminder.

ABOUT
ACTS-TENSIVE
WEALTH ACADEMY

ACTS-Tensive Wealth Academy is a financial education company that has been set up to educate and empower more individuals, including youths and adults, in financial literacy.

Founded by Joanne Lai, an accredited financial counsellor who has been passionate about financial planning since a young age, the Academy aims to help people achieve financial wellness and financial freedom. It leverages on Joanne's decade-long experience on educating individuals, and reaches out to people and families of all ages and from all walks of life, to help them grow their wealth through sound financial principles.

The Academy is so named because part of the profits earned from the company will be used to extend service to the underprivileged.

A = Acquire and
C = Create Wealth for
T = Transformation of Lives and
S = Service to Others

WORKSHOPS

The Academy runs a number of workshops that deal with different financial topics, catering to a wide range of people. Here we provide snippets of what these are. For more information and to sign up, please visit our website at: **https://acts-tensive-wealth-academy.com** or call (65) 6222-1156.

Start Your First Teen-Investment Account
An enlightening session for both teenagers and parents that gets them talking about Money, a topic most find difficult to discuss. It helps them to develop the right mindset about money, savings, and investments.

Be a Master Investor

Learn how to develop a Midas touch for your investments through this workshop. It will equip you with the essentials to understand financial jargon and cycles, pick the right investments for yourself, avoid scams and most of all, sleep well at night while your investments grow.

Build Your Private ATM and Retirement Portfolio

This workshop will help you design your own ATM, one that can pay you monthly regardless of the economic situation. It will also provide tips on how to shock-proof your investment portfolio and leave a meaningful legacy for your loved ones.

Leaving a Lasting Legacy

If you have not had your will done but want to ensure that your hard-earned money goes to those you care about, then this is the presentation for you. Find out what really happens to your estate after you pass on and how you can write a simple yet good will to protect your assets.

Good Debts, Bad Debts

Discover the 4S's—sheltering, spending, savings, shielding—that will allow you to finance your dreams and keep out of debt.

Financial Literacy, Financial Intimacy

Men and women approach finances differently. Understanding this and getting it to work to a couple's advantage is the key to financial stability in the home.

Romancing and Financing Your Dream Home

Home ownership is a long-term financial commitment. Attend this talk to find out how to finance your dream home, protect and bequeath it, as well as make a return on your investment.

ABOUT THE AUTHOR

Joanne Lai started her own financial planning at the age of 14, and was so successful that she paid for her own university education. Fully aware that financial wellness is within everyone's grasp, she has dedicated herself to helping others achieve the financial stability that she has.

Joanne has more than ten years of experience in financial planning with IPP financial advisors. She specialises in comprehensive financial planning, particularly in investments, estate planning, and will writing. She has won numerous prominent awards and even attained the prestigious Certified Financial Planner (CFP), acclaimed to the be gold standard in financial planning. Over the years, she has partnered with many MNCs, SMEs, and hospitals to conduct educational talks for a wide range of people and guide them through the efficient use of their personal finances.

Caring for the underprivileged is one of Joanne's main reasons for living and she volunteers her time partnering with *The Straits Times School Pocket Money Fund* to teach underprivileged youth about financial management. As an Accredited Financial Counsellor and Financial Educator, she sets aside time to help people get out of dept in Singapore and Vietnam, creating opportunities for the poor to achieve financial wellness. Using financial resources garnered from her own dividend and rental income, she set up an ACTS Fund in Hue, Vietnam, for the underprivileged people.

9 789811 141041